All Transpare ...ngs
Need Thundershirts

Dana Roeser

Winner of the Two Sylvias Press Wilder Series Book Prize

Two Sylvias Press

Two Sylvias Press
PO Box 1524
Kingston, WA 98346
twosylviaspress@gmail.com

Cover Artist: Melora Griffis, *extra*, 2015, mixed media 12 x 12 in.
Cover Design: Kelli Russell Agodon
Book Design: Annette Spaulding-Convy
Author Photo: Donald Platt

Created with the belief that great writing is good for the world, Two Sylvias Press mixes modern technology, classic style, and literary intellect with an eco-friendly heart. We draw our inspiration from the poetic literary talent of Sylvia Plath and the editorial business sense of Sylvia Beach. We are an independent press dedicated to publishing the exceptional voices of writers.

For more information about Two Sylvias Press please visit: www.twosylviaspress.com

First Edition. Created in the United States of America.

ISBN: 978-1-948767-06-4

Two Sylvias Press
www.twosylviaspress.com

Praise for *All Transparent Things Need Thundershirts*

Dana Roeser's voice—hilarious, tragic, musical, transcendent—announces itself in the title of this collection, and in every line to follow. This is work that is deceptively skilled, written by a poet with a sure hand, a sense of comic timing as well as of the abrupt, stabbing surprise, with an ear for the music of our language and mastery of her poetry's artwork—precisely intricate, finely wrought, and so purely achieved that it becomes as transparent as all things magically invisible but vibrantly animate, echoing and mocking and illuminating the transparencies of this collection's title. To read this poetry is to appreciate not only the talent of this poet, but to feel renewed in one's faith in poetry itself. How exciting to discover this voice—kind, profane, pure, and honest—and to be moved and changed, amused and reassured, frightened and satisfied and reunited with one's own experiences and one's own lost selves through an encounter with poems made out of authenticity, wit, intelligence, and generosity.

—Laura Kasischke

༄

Let's say you almost lost your sight but instead you went to the doctor and the procedure saving your vision is so commonplace you wouldn't even go so far to call it a miracle. Let's say that experience was nothing more or less miraculous than having fiercely loved one's fragile children, or riding a horse in circles around a ring, or buying a ticket to ride in a chair thousands of miles across the sky, or feeding your dying father the single red grape he has been craving. Let's say you are a poet and rather than dressing up the daily vulnerabilities of addiction, aging, recovery, and fear with poetic devices and rhetorical flares, you used the same tenor and diction you always use to describe your life. Would it be a miracle if those words struck a reader like a hot flash of raw, lyrical intensity and beautiful honesty? Yes, it would be a miracle and also it would be a book, this very one in fact, which you could carry in your pocket and read over and over again, anytime the astonishments of being alive started to wear off.

—Kathryn Nuernberger

༄

Dana Roeser is a poet of scrupulous, momentary attention, of emotions that rush at each other from the depths of pathos and the heights of exultation. These emotions do not collide but coexist by virtue of a high colloquial style that seems to move effortlessly from hyperbole to understatement. But make no mistake: as we travel from hairdresser to hospice to dressage ring, a crisis is being braved. In sixteen elegant, fearless, heartbreaking, and often hilarious poems, Roeser marks the stations of her personal cross. Few poets have set more life in motion and achieved such heroic balance. *All Transparent Things Need Thundershirts* is a wonder.

—Rodney Jones

Acknowledgments

Thanks to the editors of the following publications, in which these poems, sometimes in slightly different versions, first appeared:

Denver Quarterly: "His Chemic Beauty"

Green Mountains Review: "A Tour of Pauline Hot Spots in Malta, in Which I Boast of My Humiliations" and "Flying Change"

GMR Online: "Dental Work/Shiny Object"

Iowa Review: "How God Is like a Truffle"

Laurel Review: "Cindy from Marzahn on the Night of the Mayan Apocalypse"

Mississippi Review: "Figure, Ground"

Pleiades: "Twenty-Meter Circle"

Poetry: "Transparent Things, God-Sized Hole"

Prairie Schooner : "Crush"

Seneca Review: "My Hobby Needed a Hobby"

Southern Humanities Review: "The Inn at Tallgrass"

Southern Review: "Letter to Dr. M." and "Poem Starting with Dry Cleaning"

Southwest Review: "Pool"

Sou'wester: "The Fire Academy"

"My Hobby Needed a Hobby" was reprinted in the *Pushcart Prize XLIII* (2018).

"The Fire Academy" was reprinted in *Privacy Policy, The Anthology of Surveillance Poetics*, Ed. Andrew Ridker, Black Ocean Press (2014).

"The Fire Academy" was also reprinted in *Not like the Rest of Us: An Anthology of Contemporary Indiana Writers,* Eds. Barbara Shoup and Rachel Sahaidachny, INwords/Indiana Writers Center (2016).

My deepest thanks go to Suzanne Cleary, Alessandra Lynch, and Mary-Sherman Willis for their attention to these poems/this project and their unstinting encouragement. Special thanks to Donald Platt.

My thanks also to these compassionate poet-editors: Wyn Cooper, Sarah Green, and Amelia Martens (of Black Lawrence Press), who helped me to see this book as a reader would. I am indebted to the kind people willing to supply commentary for the book: Rodney Jones, Laura Kasischke, and Kathryn Nuernberger.

The Ragdale Foundation and VCCA France (Moulin à Nef) provided residencies that greatly aided in the completion of this manuscript. Thank you to Ross White, founder of The Grind, for which many of these poems were written and revised. I would also like to express my gratitude for encouragement and support, of the deep psychic kind, to S.S., P.D., and K.B. And for her expertise as trainer, of both horses and riders, and for her friendship, to Christy Weigle.

Thank you to Melora Griffis, for the use of her mixed media work, *extra*, which is featured on the book's cover. I greatly appreciate Daschielle Louis's input on the cover's design.

I'd like to acknowledge Arthur Kern, the artist who created the horse sculptures mentioned in the poem "Dental Work/Shiny Object."

In the poem "Cindy from Marzahn on the Night of the Mayan Apocalypse," the words of Ilka Bessin (aka "Cindy from Marzahn") were translated from the German by Portia Rutherford.

And, finally, I owe a debt of gratitude to Kelli Russell Agodon and Annette Spaulding-Convy of Two Sylvias Press for choosing this book and for being so lovely to work with.

Table of Contents

ॐ

For Don, Eleanor, and Lucy

For Doug

In memory of Karin Kooreman (1959-2013)
and Erwin Roeser (1922-2015)

LETTER TO DR. M.

Dear Dr. Maddingly, I'm writing
        to let you know I took

seriously your admonition
        not to go running for at least

three weeks until whatever the
        vitreous jelly stuff that's

making those gray shadows tree branches
        flashing lights in the peripheral

vision of my right eye gets settled. In order
        to prevent serious retinal problems

that require surgery. I did the
        following alternate exercises:

riding—you did say I could
        go riding—my friends and I laughed

at the stable about how you probably
        OK'd riding because you don't

know what it *is*. Most people
        seem to think it's sitting on a

horse! Ha ha! We love picturing
        those people on a horse—or

my favorite—we love picturing
        our bosses on horses!

How about riding a horse
        in a tornado? I forgot to

ask about that. Restraining the
        horse I just hopped

off of during the actual
        blast as she stood on her

hind legs and waved her
        forelegs. (I was in an indoor

arena, a barn—that counts for
        something, right?) Or tornadoes

in general. Or rescuing
        horses in a debris-strewn

windy pasture in the dark
        after. Who are hysterical

and afraid. I hear today
        the other side of the

arena was "badly damaged"—
        would that be "torn off"? I didn't

even see it, though I heard
        a splintering crashing noise

that activated the
        "This could be it" idea. My

therapist asked what I was
        thinking. I said I was concentrating

on taking care of Ruth's beloved
        Vaydran, who is a pet who is

sweet, if obsessed with food,
        and was frightened. I think

I thought I might end up under
        a pile of lumber (my personal

euphemism, I guess) with her.
        And I thought okay but was

ashamed that I had for this
        one stupid time only not been

vigilant about warnings and even
        more ashamed later when I

learned there had been twenty-five-plus
        tornadoes in my area. That's when

I learned shame would
        probably be with me

at my death—my
        default setting. Saliva

tears snot and the sense that
        I'd done something irreparable.

The other thought in there
        somewhere was that my accounts

were cleared, fairly, and "my
        side of the street" was

clean. You see I was thinking
        of my friend Karin who lay

in cardiac critical care
        on life support—but with her

(heavily sedated) brain intact—
        I was pretty ass angry about

that and not thinking one
        speck about my retina

and its goo.
        And then, Zumba—you didn't

mention. I did it Saturday
        after I'd learned about the induced

coma and today
        after I learned she had died.

I went to Indianapolis to see her
        yesterday. I forgot about

my retina! I swear
        she knew me——my voice——

and was responding with
        her eyebrows forehead

and chin. Had the nurses lightened
        up her pain meds, or . . . ? I told

her I thought she would
        make it. Denial has

its value though it does
        make me forget to baby

my eye and to think
        strictly of the letter of

the law rather than
        the spirit when it comes

to your restrictions. Zumba is
        fantastic! It is pure joy.

I knew it was the totally
        right thing both times I

went. I tried not to jump.
        I did the tossing yes

and a lot of pelvic
        thrusting——fabulous——

it made me think of when
        I was twenty and took modern dance

in a storefront on Magazine
                Street in New Orleans with

a six-four sexy guy teacher and a live
                conga drummer. My legs were

so long—as tonight—it
                took me a split second

longer to swing them around
                and up and down and I had to

compensate. The whole street
                could see us and I didn't care.

I'm in that mood now
                too. Sixty and going to

get a shorter haircut so I can do more
                sweaty things and wash it

in the shower anytime I
                feel like it. So I can smell

like horse as often as I get
                the opportunity. I truly

hope the Jell-O
                is settling or recongealing

or whatever it's supposed
                to do. I'll be in to let

you shine that huge lens
                with the shocking

light behind it in there
                and have me swivel

my eye to each of the numbers
                on an imaginary

clock face to check it. Like you told
    me to do when I was

in a week ago. Only a
    week! (Look how hard

I've tried to obey.) And two more
    to go. I don't think I'll

be able to invent
    anything else to bend the

rules. Joy, Dr. M. Joy! The body!
    I love your soft hands on my

face. Your voice. I've always
    loved you. More about

that later. Yes, I'm still
    seeing a few shadow branches

and twigs dangling around
    my visual windshield. In the deep

dark of my right peripheral
    vision, some brilliant meteor showers.

Let me tell you, Tom (may
    I call you Tom?), I got lucky

twice. The tornado.
    And landing in my friend's one

conscious window. No one
    can explain that. Her sighs,

the movement of her chin,
    her raised eyebrow and

her wrinkled forehead. The
    sighs showed up on the

breathing monitor and there was
        occasionally a skipped

heartbeat ("not atypical"
        the call nurse said). Karin, I waited

for Joe, the nurse I liked,
        "your" nurse, to return from

lunch because I felt the nurse
        in the hall screwing around with

a laptop was not adequately
        solicitous. She said some woman

managed to get through on the phone
        from Michigan. The woman said you

were driving by one day
        and saw her Chow attacked

by some pit bulls—and stopped and
        saved him/her. She heard you

were ill and wanted to inquire.
        I didn't tell you. I wanted

you to myself. I inscribed a cross
        on your forehead as a priest

taught me to do a long time
        ago, then apologized—

you weren't big on God.
        I had two lucky opportunities.

In the cross hairs of
        bad weather and the Cardiac

Critical Care Unit. I don't
        know why. I don't

believe in a personal favor
        kind of god. Love

and Godspeed to you Karin.
        And Dr. M., Tom, I'll try

not to get in any more
        trouble—will take it all

in the hips, rather than jumping
        up and down, in Zumba,

and ride a horse just by sitting there
        as you must have envisioned—will

see you in two weeks, after
        the holidays, the travel,

my friend flying along beside
        me, as she did in life, I don't

doubt, and you somewhere
        waiting with your clock face,

your lovely kind voice and
        soft steady hands, peering

into my eyes' dark depths
        with your "opthalmoscope," I

just found out it's called, its
        searching magnifying light.

POEM STARTING WITH DRY CLEANING

If I don't hurry and pick up
    that dry cleaning
she's going to give it away;
    surely it's been over a month
by now—the dress is
    sleeveless. I'm going
to swerve in there and make
    myself late for
Zumba, to be a good
    dry-cleaning-picking-
up citizen, but then I realize
    with their shorter
hours, I've missed
    it again. I hate these
people, their business failing;
    they keep making
it impossible for the
    rest of us.

Please Lord, where did
    I get this mouth
on the front of my head. I've
    got to get back
to church. Twelve-step is
    not quite doing it, as
I keep falling in
    love with the bad
boys, or *one* bad boy, I should
    say. Enough about
the oral surgeon.

    Back to argument
with self about
    horseback riding about
how I should call and
    cancel because I am
still tired from my trip and
    it's so effing cold
out there. But then, No,
    listen, doll, if you

start cancelling
        you won't go, then
you'll lose your muscles
        and it won't
be safe to go
        but really if you
don't go you'll lose
        the big scoops
of fresh air and wind,
        of long grass
and horses' manes, of
        stampeding horses
and you standing completely
        still while they
open then shut
        in a mass
continuing to
        run
around you. You'll
        miss the easy
friendship with
        Christy between
piles of excrement,
        picking
hooves, or whatever.
        Our casual
back-and-forth
        banter last summer
while she bathed
        I forget whom
and groped
        around his
sheath with her hand
        scooping out the
smegma.

        The thing with
        diurnal
journal-type
        occasional poems
is that one does
        get tired. Let

me just say this
        one thing. My father
had a scab on his
        head that looked
like it could be
        infected, like
cradle cap or
        something. He
sat in his darkened
        bedroom that reeked
of urine, going
        through files. He said
he needed to
        throw things
away.
        Finding
him there, I reminded
        myself he cannot
smell—it's part of
        Parkinson's. Still,
I was mad the people at
        the assisted-living
place weren't making
        more of
an effort. They come
        in twice
a day to change
        his catheter
bag—and also to
        check his blood
sugar and give
        him meds. Can't they
do something?
                I saw
        a huge open
nail clipper
        in the wooden
tray he keeps
        on the seat
of his walker. He asked
        me to cut
his fingernails. I hesitated,

not wanting
to hurt him. But he
            said Doug my brother
is impatient (he
            also has
a nasty alcoholic
            tremor but
I didn't bring
            that up) and
no one else
            would do it.
So I took
            his soft hands
and clipped
            one finger
at a time, the cut
            slivers sometimes
ricocheting to
            the ceiling. Then
I got an emery board
            out of the
top left drawer of
            his dresser
and smoothed down
            the edges. I went
in the kitchen
            and chopped
the celery my husband
            bought him the
other day into bite-sized pieces
            and put them
in plastic to-go
            containers he'd
saved from the
            dining room.
He handed me two
            files that were
sitting by the phone
            in his
living room. In them,
            pictures of his
mother and father.

One where
his father
        looks entirely
disheveled
        and drunk (he
died when my
        father, the
youngest of nine, was
        five, of
"not taking
        care of
himself") and another
        where he is
wearing a tight-fitting
        uniform and
has his hair
        orderly and
slicked down.
        I had never
seen that
        picture. Group shots
of my father
        with his brothers
and sisters carefully
        labeled on
the back. (My mother's
        half-brother
had my father
        investigated when
she wanted to marry
        him because
he seemed so
        "unsuitable," read,
poor—and my
        mother's father
disowned her). My father
        doesn't do
much now. When
        I said goodbye,
I bent almost
        to his waist so
I could look up

       into his pale
and exhausted
       blue eyes
behind his smeared glasses.

FLYING CHANGE

Sally, our dog,
guarded the
foot
of the stairs.
"Tell your
boyfriend
to be
careful descending
that she
doesn't
leap at
him."
Ashes
are ready
for pick-up,
her paw print
in a ceramic
disc. "We're
not going to
Vegas," the manic
pilot said. "We
need to take a
leap of
faith." Then
he yelled
over the radio
for air traffic
control to
be quiet, dimmed
the monitors,
and started
making jumbled
remarks
about Jesus, September
11th, Iraq,
Iran
and terrorists.

"She is

almost certainly
back on lithium
        judging by
her voice
        on the phone," my
friend Grace
        e-mails.
"I will pray for
        your daughter
while I pray
        for mine." She
guarded the bottom
        of the stairs
at night and
        by day
the front
        door. If the
door was open,
        even if
the outer glass
        door
was shut, we'd receive
        no mail. The next
day we'd
        get a note:
"Sorry
        we could not
deliver your mail
        yesterday. Door
was open." ("Dog,"
        implied.)

                Two
flying lead
        changes
and I was breathless.
        Nearly asthmatic.
I sat steady, steered
        Drummer straight
on the diagonal
        across the
ring and applied

leg. He knew
the signal. He was
      able to do
it front and back
      at once. Because
he'd had his
      bute that
morning.
      When the
agitated
      captain
left the cockpit
      to go to the
bathroom, the copilot let
      an off-duty
officer who was
      present
on the flight
      into the
breach and
      locked the
door. He implored
      the passengers
over the PA
      to tackle
the errant one,
      who was running
up and down
      the aisle
shouting
      and throwing
himself
      against the door.

Grace says,
      "The boyfriend
has no job . . . . He says
      he'll bring
in money as soon
      as he gets
the 'medical' marijuana
      crop going

in the garage. . . . *Sheesh!"*
        Grace remembers
my frantic
        messages about
Eleanor. She's quit
        school; she's packed
two blankets
        in her suitcase. She's
booked a flight
        but can't move
from the
        center
of her bed.

        "Are
        you still
getting some juice
        out of it?" asked
my neighbor Danny
        when I told
him about my guilt
        over putting
the dog
        down.
She was throwing
        her head
to the sky in
        her seizure,
she was swimming
        all over
the living
        room floor. "She
guarded us." We need
        to get a
locksmith over
        now that
she's not here. How
        long will it
take for the people
        who watch
to notice
        she is gone?

He was removed
        from the
plane in
        what was
essentially
        a strait-
jacket. In the struggle,
        he bruised
a flight
        attendant's
ribs. "He was suffering
        from a
'medical condition.'"
        Our daughter's taking
another
        gap year . . .
to the
        highlands
of Guatemala. We're not
        paying.
I go to NAMI
        and I
go to Al-Anon.
        "Will the 'Landscape
Fabric' block
        the earthworms
from coming up
        from beneath
into the
        raised bed?"
I write to Jody. She
        replies,
"Earthworms
        are an exotic
species not
        native to
Indiana." As though
        that were
relevant
        to the earth cloth
question. They
        will fly

down from the
        sky, Danny
says of seed mote—
        as if it
contained the egg cases
        of earthworms
and segmented circular grubs.
        Danny and
I look at the violets
        on the grass
inside the
        wooden walls
of the empty raised
        bed and
decide I should
        skip it. "The
wood will rot,"
        he says happily. "The whole
thing will rot."

        Her pristine
body was at
        the vet
over the weekend
        before
they could
        send it
off to "Pet
        Remembrance." Whatever
the crematorium
        is named. (I knew
where she'd rubbed
        her "elbows"
bare from lying
        on the
hardwood
        floor.) "The ashes
are ready for
        pick-up,"
said Donna
        the receptionist.
I felt like my

                    head,
my analytic thing,
                    separated
from my emotion/
                    sopping self when I
made the decision.
                    I can't
get the
                    two in
concert.
                    Danny said, "I
think everybody
                    feels that." I said
"I think this
                    is why
I can't hold
                    a job." "Are
you still getting
                    mileage
out of that?" Violets
                    dotted the
whole gorgeous
                    rotting backyard.

I stood, cold, my
                    sleep culottes
with the stretched-out
                    waistband
bunched in my hand,
                    a twenty-year-
old sweater over
                    my faded
sleep shirt. I'd run
                    out to talk to Danny
while he was
                    feeding the
feral cats (whom
                    he named
a few years
                    back after
his favorite
                    jazz greats—

Fats Navarro, Cole
             Porter, Horace
Silver.) He
             said, "I'll
move my
             mulch pile
so the
             Soilmaker
truck can get in."
             I said, "You're
wearing a pack."
             He said, "It's
true, I'm wearing
             a pack. But
I'll be back. You
             said the truck
is coming at
             four."

Louis C.K., in his
             stand-up routine
on YouTube, pre-#MeToo,
             "Everything's
Amazing &
             Nobody's
Happy," says, "People complain
             'We had
to sit there
             on the runway
for 40 minutes.' . . . Oh
             really? And then
what happened next?
             Did you *fly*
through the *air*
             like a *bird?*"
When she
             had the
seizure
             panting, her
eyes darting
             side to
side, the sudden

paroxysms
upward as though
        she
were trying
        to get
up, it was like
        she was
flying, one wing
        listing badly, gravity
proving more
        nettlesome than
usual. The flying
        lead change.
My teacher said, "Now
        cut across
the arena and
        change direction."
This thundering
        you feel underneath
you, as the horse
        accelerates,
the entr'acte while
        he makes
the change.

        Eleanor's mind was going
so fast, I think,
        she couldn't
breathe, or
        move. She asked
me to breathe
        with her
one nostril at a
        time
over the
        telephone.

Several
        off-duty security
people were
        on the plane.
As it happened,

they were
going to a security
                convention in
the destination
                city. They held
the erratic pilot down
                until the copilot
and the off-duty
                guy he'd recruited
could land the
                plane in
Amarillo, Texas. "A
                medical condition. . . . The
issue of pilot health . . .
                is
longstanding."
                "So my fingers
are crossed," Grace said.
                "While I was praying
for my daughter,
                I threw
in some prayers
                for yours." When
Don got there,
                he discovered
she had tied
                a blouse
and a scarf
                to the fifth-
floor fire escape
                outside her
apartment window. She
                begged him
to let her
                go out and
release them
                over the
park.

                "Life
is amazing
                and people

aren't happy. . . .
         You're flying
from New York
         to California
in five *hours?* That used
         to take
thirty years! A bunch
         of you would
die on
         the way and have
babies——you'd
         be a whole
different
         group of people
when you got
         there. . . . Everybody
on every plane
         should be
going, 'Oh my God.
         Wow!' You're
sitting
         in a chair
in the *sky*!"

TRANSPARENT THINGS, GOD-SIZED HOLE

All transparent things need
          thundershirts. The little
ghost hanging from an eave,
          on Underwood
Street, a piece of
          lavender-tinted
netting stretched onto
          a metal frame. The Boston
terriers and Chihuahuas patiently
          wait out storms
with their eyes bulging
          in their special
wraparound shirts. My
          family used to
laugh at me
          sleeping under
two down quilts, wearing a wool
          hat in summer,
when I said
          I was afraid
otherwise I would
          fly up to the ceiling.

Once on a sidewalk
          beside Erie Street
around the corner
          from Underwood
where the pointless
          obsolete
tracks run to a dead end
          on the other side,
I found a black
          and silver rosary,
with shining
          onyx beads, like
the ones
          that you see
hanging
          from the belts of

nuns in their habits or priests
            in their chasubles.
I kept it
            carefully until either
I lost it or it got buried
            in the bottom of a purse
abandoned under
            my bed or in the
closet. Clutter keeps
            me bound to this
earth.
            I told Patti last night
            that the God-sized
hole in me was
            so big and vacant,
voracious and spacious,
            it was like I was
running some kind
            of desperate toddler's
shape-sorter game, trying to find
            something that fit
to plug into it. I'd stuff anything
            in there, regardless
of whether the shape
            coincided with
the opening. It was
            like I could look
at the sky and attract
            space junk, broken
satellites, spent rocket
            stages,
micrometeoroids, to
            plug the
gap.

            The wind is its own
kind of chaos,
            sometimes like a sheet
of itself tangled
            or flowing
on a celestial
            clothesline. It needs

a weighted blanket.
        Little red flags
on the maple
        at the corner of
Underwood and Erie
        near the switching yard.
Slow-moving locomotives
        that might be driven by
nobody. Flags
        hold the tree down,
mark it, make it know
        it's real.
Flapping on the flaming maple
        or falling.

CINDY FROM MARZAHN ON THE NIGHT
OF THE MAYAN APOCALYPSE

On the night of
the end of the world
I had a vigorous
Chinese massage—
forty minutes including
reflexology—
in a cordoned-
off area in the center
of the walkway
across from the Hickory
Farms kiosk in the
Tippecanoe Shopping Mall
in Lafayette,
Indiana. It was
just after
sunset on the shortest
day of the
year. Lying
there,
fully clothed (except
for my feet
and calves—the masseuse
took off
my socks
and pushed
up my leggings),
I was
approximately 80%
myself,
like that woman,
"Cindy from
Marzahn," welfare
recipient
from East Berlin, in
The Times today,
who said her stand-up
comic self
comes in at approximately

80% of her
"actual" self, Ilka Bessin.

My personal
effects in two white
        plastic receptacles
just below my downward-
        pointing face,
my coat thrown over
        a folding chair. People
could have swept by
        and robbed me—
of keys, credit card,
        bobby pins,
barrettes, of the Swarovski
        crystal
necklace I asked my daughter
        to get my husband
to buy me last
        Valentine's Day.

                        I wish
I could tell you
        that exposing
my personhood
        this way
nearly sixty years old and
        clothed in copious winter
layers under fluorescent
        lights
with secularized Christmas music
        blaring from
the public
        address system, occasionally
peering through
        the face rest
at the linoleum floor,
        getting
karate-chopped and brutally
        kneaded by a tiny
Asian woman,
        could have

~ 30 ~

conferred the
            "ego strength"
Katherine keeps
            referring to
that would
            fit me
for my new
            life after
the apocalypse—
            of disappointment,
unemployment, knee
            blowout, back
kink, aged-out
            obsolescence,
irrelevance,
            almost
unbearable worry
            about my
children,
            etc. Make
me viable. Not
            like before,
as, yes, that was
            pretty much
imagined, but
            as never before.

Ilka became
            "Cindy" by
mistake; she'd called
            a comedy club
for a job as a receptionist
            and while she was reciting
her woes, the manager
            stopped her
and invited her
            to audition
to be a stand-up!

            You gotta love
that manager, O Naked One.
            Sex-Thrasher.

When Ilka was
        just Ilka,
before she became
        "Cindy," her
80% representation,
        after however
many ignored
        résumés, she sank
into the sofa and
        the overweight
of her invisibility,
        where anything
went because
        nothing did.
She was waiting
        for something—
black helicopter,
        silver drone,
the Four Horsemen
        of the
Apocalypse,
        maybe a Pleiadian
clusterfuck. She was waiting
        for something—
when she rose
        up as Cindy
she was wearing
        a too-tight pink
spangled sweatsuit, a giant
        plastic peony
in her over-permed
        hair. A thick
layer of
        makeup with
brown lip liner.
        "The reason
I'm here today
        is because the
people who called me
        said, 'Cindy,
we need a little more
        sex appeal

in the performance. . . .'
        And now I'm here.
Actually, I'm not doing
        so well. Excuse
me. I don't
        have a job.
But I've completed
        my course studies
and I finally know
        why I don't
have a job. I am
        simply too
good-looking. The problem
        is that
in the rejection letters
        I receive,
they always say, 'Miss
        Cindy,
you have to work on
        your looks
a little bit.' What am
        I supposed to
do? Should I make
        myself look
ugly or what?"

        I reconstructed myself
in coat, scarf, mohair beret,
        Valentine's
necklace, on and under
        the folding chairs,
naked in my
        layers, invisible, as
only postmenopausal
        women can
be, in the center
        of the heavily
trafficked aisle
        in the Tippecanoe
County Mall
        four days
before the birth

of Jesus or
facsimile, on the
        possible actual last
night of
        the world.
Threading
        the gauntlet
of "Smoked Cheddar
        Blend"
and garish red
        salami, "Spiral Sliced
Honeygold Ham" and
        "Sesame,
Caraway & Sea Salt
        Crackers,"
princess cut
        diamond
engagement rings and
        tennis bracelets:
exorbitant "push"
        presents
glittering in the glass
        case of Fred
Layton Jeweler,
        and out Exit E
to the frigid
        parking lot, rows
of car hoods
        idling under
greenish streetlights.
        Disappointed
and thrilled. The
        pavé diamonds
of frost pressing
        down on
those hulks. No signs
        of the apocalypse,
locusts banging
        into my face
lashing me with
        the tails
of scorpions. Just the

                    frost-covered cars
brooding under the
                    pale green
energy-saver
                    streetlights. And
Cindy out there
                    somewhere
with her
                    80 or
her 100% self.
                    Somebody
standing on a crescent
                    moon with
a crown of stars
                    over by the bus
stop.

FIGURE, GROUND

How many times
        do I have to
hear that the figures
        in Matisse's
paintings meant no more
        to him than
the ground, that
        shapes were simply
shapes; colors, feelings;
        and "accuracy"
was not a goal? He added
        the vertical
slats of a balcony railing,
        thin horizontal
shutters on a made-up
        window,
to add interest
        in *The Yellow*
Dress. He had been stuck on
        it for two years.
He traveled to
        Tahiti. He traveled
to the U.S., knew what
        to do when he
finally returned home.
        In the case of
the *Large Reclining*
        Nude, he ended up
adding a checkered
        blue background and
refining the woman's shape
        into something
abstracted, nearly
        grotesque. And there
is a lot of figure/
        ground intermingling
in *Still Life,*
        Bouquet of
Dahlias

and White Book. The arc
of the flower stems is
        echoed in vase, chair, fruit,
pink peony blossom
        on the screen behind.
As in *Purple Robe*
        and Anemones,
again and again it
        is emphasized
by the commentators on the
        audio, on the placards,
the docent,
        that Henri did not
care who the model was or
        whether his representation
resembled her—whether
        flowers encroached upon
the figure of the sitter
        as in the aptly titled
Romanian Blouse
        with Foliage.

                        I came to the
museum straight
        from the hospital.
I traded the monochromatic
        Cardiac Critical
Care Unit 2205
        with its easy-
to-hose-down tile,
        its machines
and pumps and tubes,
        the jaundiced
face of my
        friend poking
above a sheet
        that encased
her like a sarcophagus,
        for the sun-drenched
colors of the
        Mediterranean,
Nice, Morocco.

They were
the same:
        the room
with its curtain
        tracks
in the ceiling
        for bed
and toilet, each,
        not that my
friend would any
        day soon
be needing
        the latter.
Her heart
        was outside
her body—past
        her feet—
two metal
        boxes, one
labeled "Left,"
        the other
"Right." Several clear
        tubes were
coiled
        brilliant red—
her blood. Presumably,
        under the tucked-
in sheet, many
        of the tubes and
wires were hooked
        up. Yet, she
was *not* in a
        coma. She knew
who I was from
        the get-go,
and she listened to
        every word. Joe
the nurse showed me
        the dialysis
machine, "dialysis lite,"
        he called it, for
my friend's blood pressure

was too low
for the heavier variety.
        He said, The idea
is a heart and kidney
        transplant
in one—down the
        road, when
she is better.
        On her waxen
head, her
        hair was
lank and nearly
        colorless, except
for the dyed bits
        further down
on her head
        on the pillow.
She had a feeding
        tube inserted in
a nostril, a ventilator hose
        down her
throat. My friend's
        body spread
farther than her
        body, into
the pattern of the room.
        A stretch to make
it *Purple Robe*
        and Anemones,
The Yellow Dress,
        or *Romanian Blouse*
with Foliage?

        The fact
that my friend's body
        extended to the
far corners of
        her allotted
rectangle, that
        she wasn't
adhering to
        conventions,

did not diminish her.
            Rather
the room was
            charged—
figure, ground/ground,
            figure. Ventilator;
dialysis machine;
            metal
boxes: chambers
            of the heart;
black background
            with white
crosshatching; the seated
            model a
series of
            curves;
her attempt
            to lift
her head, to
            turn it. I thought
I saw her raise
            an eyebrow, wrinkle
her forehead. Red
            dahlias encroaching
on flower-print
            wallpaper, trying
to get at
            the white
book: her
            three internal
bleeds.

THE FIRE ACADEMY

I want to be a student
        at the Fire Academy
and not, as in
        my dream last
night, the gassing
        practicum. Why
did we all sit there,
        obediently,
in our detachable
        desks, new carpet
smell, gas seeping
        in, in that
sunken classroom,
        instead of fleeing?
It wasn't until the
        very end that
it occurred
        to me to not
wait for permission,
        to go. To gather
up the high school students
        in the "gathering
area" and whatever
        we were, teachers
in training—some
        version of
grad students. One woman
        had already
escaped. She heard the
        lecture, she saw
the list, and she
        said, Excuse me,
uh, I just have to
        go do something.

Blue spruce.
        Like a flash
of fire. Very tall. I forgot
        to look the

one time I was
         there since
twenty-five years
         ago, at the
side yard. There was
         so much
to look at, my childhood
         house. Inhabited
by a music professor—and
         his wife and
the yipping schnauzers. He
         let me in! (His
wife wasn't
         home!) He
let me into the
         "elevator game"
hallway back
         behind the
kitchen, with its
         five doors.
But not upstairs.
         Dreams take
place all around
         there, even near
the split rail
         fence (surely
that's gone) near
         the spruce. A
display of
         Christmas trees.
We got them
         from the tree farm
each year with a
         ball of dirt. Do they
never die?

         Here, there's a spruce
tree back
         behind an
abandoned
         furniture
store—or is it not

                    abandoned?
I can't quite remember.
                    I know more than
half the retail "spaces"
                    in that mall
are empty—
                    and there
are cracks and
                    exuberant
bursts of weed in
                    the parking
lots. Not universally. Just
                    in places. My favorite
is when a drive
                    has been built,
a feeder
                    road to some
prospective
                    business—a "pain
clinic," a medical
                    supply store,
an advance-on-your-
                    tax-return-
loan-shark place—
                    paved, organized,
curved and then
                    just stopped,
cut off with
                    a knife after
five or twenty
                    feet. Nix
that project!
                    I saw the fir
tree, I mean the
                    spruce,
on a little slope
                    leading down to
a small ravine, cattails,
                    a slope up the
other side, separated by a
                    chicken wire
fence leading to

nothing, leading
to nature, trees.
            I was in
the "loading area,"
            orange back
doors
            for the mall
stores. One
            lonely car. Affair?
Drug deal?
            Loading something?
The spruce
            was flaming
though. Thriving. Screaming
            of Christmases
past. I don't think,
            though, that some
child and her
            father brought
it out there
            one
holiday-aftermath,
            in its ball
of dirt.

            The Fire
            Academy is
the place for me. High
            school kids
in the country,
            in lieu of
"cosmetology" school,
            the Lafayette
Beauty Academy,
            are training
at the Fire Academy.
            And here
they can practice
            on real fires,
as the crews are
            all volunteer
anyway. (If fire doesn't

suit them, they
can become
          EMTs.)
Where was
          it I lived
that there was
          a special
fire building
          on the
outskirts
          of town, off
of some four-lane
          semi-main-
drag? Many of
          the places
I have lived
          have been
flyover standouts.
          A four-
or five-story brick building
          sitting alone
by the road
          in some weeds. Used
for staging
          fires, death,
and destruction
          over and
over, and the fire
          students would
scramble
          up and down
the faces the
          staircases
looking for
          dummies, who
were posing
          as smoke-stricken
people or bodies.
          I used
to look at that
          place. Death
and destruction

            headquarters.
Please let me
            not state
the obvious: "If
            only it could
be restricted to
            that, to that
one building." The woman
            escaped, with
a phony excuse,
            a lie. Shall I start
with that? All the lies
            I hear all the time,
every day. There are
            so many lies
in the air, so much
            willful
obfuscation, cheating,
            why bother
looking for
            the breathable
air? As a child, I loved
            people half-heartedly,
already with a
            shield. Only
person in the
            security tent
was me. In the Fire
            Academy all
of that is
            burned off. You may
not be able
            to be heard,
but at least
            what interactions
you have
            can be trusted
to be genuine.
            Save me.
Save him. Save her.
            Get the
child. Get the cat.

Crawl on your
belly under the
        smoke. I can't
breathe. I love
        you. I'm sorry.
Something's
        strobing
me, stroking me,
        basting me,
some awful
        clean thing
that'll strop
        me like
a razor, right
        against
my skin.

CRUSH

Why do they call it "crush"?
The man strapped in horizontal

on the hydraulic lift, then tipped vertical,
bellowing, I *am* standing

up. The nurses trying to strategically
catapult him into the bathroom so he

can brush his teeth.
Greg described my dad's

menu as "mechanically softened."
They actually take the entire

rib-eye steak, or chicken parmigiana,
and put it through a meat grinder.

On Irish night, my father, uncharacteristically,
screamed, "This is revolting!

I won't eat it." Imagine corn beef and cabbage
in a paste. I heard later that the patrons

in the main dining room were
reimbursed the price

of their dinners. That's how unsavory
the entrees were even before

pulverization. I had Irish
cream shrimp. And a soaking baked potato.

&

Crush. Coup de foudre. Blow to
the head, lightning strike. It's annoying

to fall for a garden variety
womanizer with whom I have

nothing in common. And I'm not the
only one. Whole twelve-step meetings

filled with women who have washed
their hair. I feel like giving that thing

a blow to its head. But it keeps
sashaying up to me when I'm shaking

my pelvis to some pining, thrusting love song in
Zumba class—like a Cat-5 hurricane

in the Wall of Wind simulator.

&

My father begs me, I mean *begs*,
for red grapes. Red grapes, he says, or

a sip of water—his hand in a pinch—
just one. No, I want real water.

"Thickener" is put in every drink he ingests.

&

What if he breaks your heart?
my friend Cicily says, her inquiring, open

face tilted up to mine.
A moment before,

when I was extolling his charms,
"And have you seen the other

side of that?" I had to say
I had. "Yes, he is very wound up."

&

Sally was lit up like a sparkler,
her thinning gray hair every which way,

getting stupendously drunk
but still strikingly aware. She told

us how her first bone marrow transplant
didn't take and she needed to get

another one. Each time sobering up the only
match, her alcoholic brother.

Sally was holding a snifter of gin
and then glass after glass of white wine.

It had been a hard day, she said. As I was
standing to leave, she told us about

her crush (as was the case the night before
when I started in at the restaurant

with Anna and Rose, out came the crushes).
She said it had gotten so bad

she avoided going into the relevant establishment
when she saw her guy's license plate in a parking

spot. Forty years married,
and devoted to his wife. Flirting

like crazy. She was married to one
of those flirts, but somehow

she focused him. His fourth wife, twenty
years. He adored her until his ailments—

the last straw was he, a Pulitzer
Prize winner, couldn't read the

computer screen—got to him
and he shot himself on a visit home from

the assisted living place
where he had been living, basically,

without a hip. Sally was in the
other room.

&

Sally was on prednisone for years.
Between that and the forced menopause,

she had several compression fractures
in her spine. Crush. Use this

word in a sentence:
her spine was crushed.

&

In my father's room
I eat bites from a piece

of fake "coffee cake" from
his tray. They've upgraded

his diet somewhat (from
"pulverized" to "smashed," I say

in the "Care" meeting—which makes
everyone laugh). But it's too late.

He eats almost nothing.
I'm going to offer him

the sip of the water
he's not allowed to have—

today he starts Hospice
so why not start breaking the rules

right away?—but he forgets
he asked. I've been assured

Hospice is going to give "pleasure
foods" and a "comfort tray" (I can't get

a clear read of what's on this
tray, besides morphine and Ativan).

&

Grief suffuses Hoy Center
Floor 2A especially at night. From

"pulverize" to "smash." The chair
seat slides up apparently so Dad's

bathroom mate can be put in it lying down.
Then he slides down the metal frame when the

nurses tilt it upwards. There's some
maneuver he needs to do that he and

they are screaming about. I'm supposed
to keep Dad's door shut.

&

The day room
gets afternoon sun. I hear

televisions. I dreamt last night
my husband was a pile of musty

magazines, with lint and dust balls,
and my love wore a short-sleeved

policeman's shirt that was too tight and riding
up with snug blue jeans

and an expression like, I've got everything
under control here. I'll supervise.

Ha. He may as well have been wearing
a "Superego" sign—though of course his suitability

for the job was open to question.

&

The day room gets afternoon sun.
I hear televisions. (My father is past

that. He never wants to watch.) A woman
in a wheelchair (come to think of it,

they're all in wheelchairs) howls in the day
room. Sundowning has commenced

and my dad demands a wheelchair ride
to his old apartment. I don't know now that

tomorrow he'll be too sick and drugged to
ask. The day room gets afternoon sun.

It lays down panels of light (it's spring
but who would know it—it's been

unseasonably cold the whole month) on the
furniture, on the few people doing nothing

in wheelchairs (except the howler), on the
whiteboard probably, noting the day of

the week, the date, and the geographic
coordinates of the Hoy Center.

Grief suffuses the place
especially at night. This is the last

night of my dad's lunatic demands. He
wants a grape. He wants to go to the

library in the residence and read *The
Economist*. He wants his old life—

and his old routine—back. They put him into
his pressed red-checked shirt. The day room

gets afternoon sun. I am crushed
by its beauty.

A TOUR OF PAULINE HOT SPOTS IN MALTA,
IN WHICH I BOAST OF MY HUMILIATIONS

To say that the priest
in St. Paul's Pro-Cathedral, Valletta,
eschews glamour

is an egregious understatement.
His one concession to
the second (okay, third, too)

millennium was a reference
to how one could
access St. Benedict's

daily reading "on one's iPhone
or computer" and
he would be willing

to explain to
you how. Then he
proceeded to read us

today's meditation. Moderation
and more moderation,
I believe. At length. Regarding

the cellarer of the monastery,
"Let there be chosen . . .
one who is wise, of mature

character, sober, not a great eater, not
haughty, not excitable . . . .
Let him take the greatest care

of the sick, of children, of guests
and of the poor . . . ."
In short, my father—

well, not really my father;
he's not good with the sick.
He freaks out.

But his habits are moderate
and measured, his monastic
single bed with the blue

spread my mother
left him in ten years ago
when she "went to heaven"

while her double bed
in the next room
lay empty all those

years—he could have been
swimming in that luxury!
The Anglicans,

so muffled in their allegiance
to their religious "brand," their
"Queen,"

hardly speak louder
than a whisper. Hymns
are subdued, ceiling fans

whirring; crucifixes tiny
(darn those flamboyant
Catholics)—hard to even

pick out really. Décor defiantly
beige, unembellished.
Beaten down—or not—

by the Carmelite Cathedral not a
block away brimming
with elderly Maltese ladies

in conservative
print dresses
and pearls, funerals followed

by weddings—several times
a day—and bedecked
with statues and

now Christmas lights (in July)—
on the oversized virgin
out front—for the upcoming

Feast of Our Lady of Mount
Carmel—and other statues
on gold pedestals

on Old Theatre Street,
shrouded, waiting for
something to happen.

During the Anglican
service, the cannons—
or fireworks—shoot off

on Manoel—"party" island
across the way in Marsamxett Harbor
for we crave some

sort of Mediterranean
exuberance. Father Godfrey
mutters on.

I keep flashing
on (poor) St. Paul's Pro-Cathedral's
"competitor," St. John's

Co-Cathedral where
the life-sized beheading
of St. John the Baptist,

by Caravaggio, hangs. The seam
between life and
        death much

        obsessed over—by me. Regarded
a little differently, I think,
        by taxi cab

        and bus drivers
in Malta, skittering
        over oil-sheened

        curves and switchbacks,
unperturbed by steep drops or oncoming
        traffic. Everywhere I turn in

        this country it is Jesus—
and then St. Paul—and their
        miracles. They don't

        think about how
Paul said: "I will not boast about
        myself, except to tell

        you of my
humiliations."
        I ducked from Freya's

        "international" hair salon
across St. Lucia's Street
        to St. Paul's Shipwreck

        Church, another church
with an inferiority
        complex. The

        man out front
was furious. Where
        was my wrap?

I apologized profusely, said
I always carried
        one but forgot

        today because I didn't
realize I'd be
        seized with

        the desire to go in the
church after
        the hair appointment, after

        bossing around the young
(yes, she was beautiful,
        really!) Maltese woman. I knew

        she was entirely too
relaxed to do
        a precise job on my hair—

        this turned out
to be true—but
        the deeper question is: does

        it matter? All this
so-called American *precision*? The hair
        did not turn out

        orange, an outcome
that I insisted upon—so the
        main goal was

        achieved. Avoidance
of red. I said, Why do all the
        blondes on the street

        have the strawberry thing
going on, and they said, Duh, this
        will not happen to

you. We—the Maltese—have
red pigment—and suddenly
I realized this

meant I was green—
which they—and now I—knew. I pranced out
of there across the

street with
my blown-out hair (ahhh, that
was done pretty nearly

right), and the
un-uniformed "guard" of
St. Paul's Shipwreck

did not want me—but then
he changed his mind.
He got over

the salon thing,
watching those women
line up on the stoop

and smoke—and
God knows what other
Jezebel activities

over there. He told me
there were wraps
by the door. And my

cotton splashy print
dress was long,
so we were good there.

There was a piece
of Paul's wrist bone, a part of the
column where St. Paul

was beheaded. A silver
replica of his severed head
on the marble surface

below. A description of the
indentations made in the stone
below the improvised "guillotine"

by the head. I loved
Paul when I was
a child. I loved those epistles.

Eighth grade, around
there. He shipwrecked
on Malta and was

forced to stay the
winter. He brought
Christianity. According to

a link my
chiropractor in West
Lafayette, Indiana—

his office in a tiny one-floor
office-strip complex—
sent me,

St. Paul's landing spot was
always guesstimated,
but now,

according to the author of
the online article who
scrutinized the

relevant passage in the Bible
"by Luke," Acts 28,
the real landing

spot could be
discovered. He found
one of the four anchors in

some lady's house—
and Publius's probable
house too. He thinks he

knows the spot.
At church this morning
at the Anglican

pro-cathedral
I periodically obsessed about
St. Paul—I mean,

my hair—and chastised
myself for same. It's only
a flag, a flap,

a pennant, I thought,
looking at the women
around me, and one

man, sitting at a place
marked "Chancellor"
with a little

bronze placard, all of whose
hair looked better and certainly
more connected

to the realm of what
could be conceivable,
not to say

natural, than mine. They hadn't
fallen prey to
this flap

decoration thing. Though
clearly, I, with
my "blonde" locks

and black roots, had. Thank
you, hairdresser, whose name
I inhumanely

did not think
to ask. Only at
one point

did you stand up
to me. You
said, menacingly,

a big, indiscreet
hunk of my hair in
one hand

and the violet-colored
creamy ammonia-"scented"
laden paintbrush

in the other (this
was going to
be "root city"),

"Everyone does it differently." At
which point
I wanted to whimper

with helplessness,
a (moderately) vain
woman going

to the salon version of
the guillotine—no
relics from

this mess
forthcoming. I thought
all about this

during the muttering under
the fans and the
vague suspicion

that I've had at church and
in twelve-step meetings
all summer here

under massive whirring
fan heads that I am
going deaf.

I told myself, Shave it off—
if you have such confidence that
it would be better

to return to square one.
Shave it off, shave it off; rid yourself
of the flag of your

tarty disposition!
"My grace is enough for thee. My
strength finds its full scope

in thy weakness," God
said to Paul
who is featured being

thrown from his
horse, in a huge
painting

behind the altar of
the Metropolitan Cathedral
of Malta in Mdina,

                    yet another church/cathedral
dedicated to him. I used to declare to every "Paul"
            that it was

                    my very favorite name
and apart from being
            a pick-up line

                    it was the truth. At St. Paul's Bay,
around Bugibba, I think,
            my face pressed

                    to the hop-on hop-off
bus's dirty window—sunburned day-trippers
            and beachgoers

                    swarming up
and down the narrow
            stairs to the upper deck

                    behind me—I watched
scooters, swimmers
            in the water, on

                    the rocky
shore, near the place where
            St. Paul was said

                    to have been
shipwrecked. I was startled for
            a moment.

                    In a little
cove, a man and his child
            bathed a white pony in the sea.

TWENTY-METER CIRCLE

                    Lately I've been
rethinking
          "discipline," my

                    old nemesis—
"punctuality"—oh, God
          help me. In the

                    dressage ring
A and C are at
          opposite ends

                    and I am to make
a twenty-meter
          circle

                    from A past
F on the rail
          to X in the center

                    back up
to the rail
          before K and back

                    up to A,
no lumps or
          bulges. My circles

                    are like lopsided
ovals—vaguely rounded
          squares. What a

                    concept! Me and
dressage, kind of like
          me and the

                    formal poem; for
example, the sonnet! (I was once
          told by a

teacher——in
a *forms* class, that
            it would perhaps

            be better
if I did *not* attempt
            it.) Come

            to think of it,
the three poet horse-people
            that I can think

            of are into
both dressage and formalism.
            How did

            I end up
here in this
            pristine indoor

            arena (no manure
piles!) with the instructor
            who only two weeks

            ago tied
my foot in the stirrup
            to the girth with

            twine
so that I'd stop letting
            it drift back——my knee

            almost splintered?
With the letters along
            the wall to guide

            perfect
figure eights, serpentines,
            long diagonals,

and leg-yields? I envy
those people with
discipline. Let's face it.

They saw the chaos
and decided
with enough personal

curb-chain
jerking they could conquer it. I
decided I could

not compete
and fucked up
everything

I touched.
I took my assignment
seriously. Hot

mess exemplar.
Okay, enough about me and my
mother. Back to

dressage. I'm
in the ring
with Christy, blonde

slightly dissolute
sort of sixties version
of a dressage

trainer. She's
exhausted from the horse
show in Indianapolis

and a rough night
after
and is conducting

postmortem by
the gate with the young-ish students
who accompanied

her.
Or she's staring at
my right foot. "Put

it where it
feels unnatural." "Put it
in *front* of the

girth. If it
feels completely wrong
then it's right." We're inside

because it
was windy and now
the wind comes up

very hard, whacking
the corrugated
metal walls, drowning

out the formerly
comforting sound of country
music on the

barn radio and the rattle
of feed pellets going
into and out

of buckets and feed
bins. The horses' low whickering
and stomping. We're

in the center for
some reason (on the hypothetical
X!), Meaghan on Mr. Frosty,

                    black half-Percheron,
Christy on her feet
            and me on Indy. A

            high wind is
banging the flimsy
            metal walls. I think

            "Is this the 'X,'
the safe place?" But Meaghan
            says, This is where the

            rain comes
through the roof. And sure
            enough it does. In little

            sprinkles. The wind
starts banging harder, Meaghan and I go
            to the rail, and Christy

            steps out of the
arena saying,
            Just do what

            you want. It's too noisy
for me to teach. Oh gee thanks. I say to
            Kylie leaning on

            the gate, Do you think
we should
            turn the dial on the

            radio, check our
phones? The town where
            this barn is,

            or is just to the east of,
has been struck
            by several

                    violent storms
and tornadoes, I remember
          hearing. "Oh,"

                    Meaghan says,
"It'll probably be
          over soon." Hmmm.

                    I decide
being on a horse
          is not an

                    altogether bad
way to go. After cataclysmic
          metallic cracking

                    and banging
rapid BB fire of
          rain—no thunder

                    that I can hear—
that's *something*—Christy returns.
          I see some sunlight

                    through translucent
plasticky panels
          up near the

                    roof. She lets
me canter the
          maniacal horse

                    she's assigned
me to. For the first
          time. She says,

                    not reassuringly, This is
a good place to do it, he
          has nowhere

to go. And suddenly
I realize the real
        nature of Indy,

        my allotted beast. He rushes
at the canter as Christy
        told me he would. Hurries

        his short-paced steps.
He tries to cut corners
        to hurry in his spasmodic

        "rhythm."
Christy says calmly,
        He really only behaves

        with me. That's what
makes him a
        good school

        horse. *Hello?* She
says, Yeah, he rushes
        the jumps too. But

        he really throws his
head and hates
        a stronger bit. Can't do much

        with a twelve-hundred-pound
beast, she says
        cheerfully. Then

        I remember his other
spasmodic characteristics.
        He has to wear

        a muzzle
to graze because he's a compulsive
        overeater and

                  is always getting obese
getting laminitis
          messing up his

                feet. He's just basically
a wreck and I have
          fantasies

              about being his
Florence Nightingale,
          Healer of the Obsessive-Compulsive,

              the fourteen-year-old
gelding off-track thoroughbred.
          In the old days

              it was
hell for leather
          now it's the hellish

              dressage patterns or
figures or
          whatever they're

              called——on the back
of a horse that used to
          race.

              Who takes each
cross-country ride,
          Christy tells me (again,

              cheerfully), as a
competition he needs to
          get in front of——

              to go faster
and faster
          placate those

            hankering demons
always indoors
            always in

            the caving-in almost-collapsing
prefab barn in
            a thrashing wind.

THE INN AT TALLGRASS

When I started my downward
slide it had his name on it.
          Katherine said, It's the Suicide
Express. In cursive like "Donna"

or "Sally" on the side of a chipped
          boat in a weedy lot
behind a defunct "repair shop"
          by the Wabash River. It even

          has a bed of grass and
weeds sprouting from its dirt-strewn
          hull. Bed! Yikes.
Don't say that word. With his

name. I texted him and said
          there was a golf course
behind me at this
          Kansas hotel that I was

          forbidden to run on. What
I meant was, You are
          a golf course I'm
forbidden to sleep with.

On the other side of the abandoned
          boat repair shop were
giant sheds for sculls that
          the rowing team used

          and the steep wood-planked
ramp I ran up and down
          sometimes for putting
in the boats. That was Indiana. That

was years ago. But loneliness
          was a place I hove
close to. Even all those years
          with children. In my giant-

toe-box running shoes, I
visited parks I never showed them.
          Now they are gone. And for
the short term I am living away

from the graveyard
          of their childhoods. It's the
natural order of things
          for them to go. Why is it

          I can't shake my disconsolation?
My husband visits me during my visiting-
          writer job in Kansas. And I shake
all over. Because with my

pumpkin and my two bouquets
          of mums, sunflowers, and
eucalyptus, my weird "instant"
          risotto boxes

          and Pamela's baking mix
(but no bourbon or sherry, thank God),
          in the upgraded
hotel "apartment," I am returning

to what I've craved. To live alone.
          To wait for the right man.
A man, dark and sparkling, Adderall-
          addled—whose name

          is inscribed on the boat
of my undoing, for example—to come
          along so we can
settle down and have a child. What is his

name but Grief? Loss of the job
          I held and loved for
years; of my treasured father; of
          Eleanor and Lucy, my daughters.

DENTAL WORK/SHINY OBJECT

Looking into my
father's dead mouth I get
a good look at
all that expensive
dental work,
the silver fillings,
bridgework,
crowns, implants etc.
he had installed
over the
years. After
a childhood
of neglect, he
was very
conscientious about
his teeth—even going
so far
as to use
a waterpik.

The dead open
mouth which
I arrived in time
to see, given
that I missed the other
bit, put me in
mind of my friend
the cosmetic
prosthodontist. Talk
about expensive! Caps,
veneers, and whatever. And
then the
reconstructive
surgery,
implantology, etc.
As it is I
wonder how my own
crowns, teeth-colored
composite fillings—

to replace the
mercury ones—and so on
will fare in
the grave, or in the crucible
of the crematorium—
in twelve
or fourteen
hundred degree
heat for two
and a half
hours.

I had an
art teacher
my freshmen
year in college
when I—surprise—
was too lazy
technically
to "prevail" as an
art major. I hated
those pencil
contour drawings
but felt
the call of
paint,
the desire to
squeeze it
from the tube, squeegee
it across
the canvas with
a palette
knife. I went in his
studio once
about some
assignment and
there were
horses lying around
on the floor,
full-sized and
exhausted,
cast in white

polyester resin.

        But back to the
teeth and my lost
        "transitional object," the
dentist. Perhaps to sell
        the product
or for better
        persuasiveness
with women in general,
        he's incredibly
well-maintained—
        the shiny sports car the
leather jackets
        the buzz cut
clipped just five
        minutes ago.
The pressed dry-
        cleaned trousers
or tight jeans the
        collars the
boots—
        I could
describe every
        outfit I've seen
him in, the rolled
        edges of the
collar and cuffs
        of the yellow
sweater—the skin—
        and don't forget
the teeth—
        he is one
big monument
        to materiality. And
I want to
        lick him all
over.

        I do lick my
        father all
over, practically, when

he is dead—his
skin is slightly acrid,
            tastes of
sawdust. I kiss
            him in
the same hollow
            of his cheek
over and over, mussing
            the scruff on
the back of his
            head, pulling
down his sheet.
            Take photos of
his hands. Pocket
            the Timex, for
which I had gone to
            great
trouble to
            get a new
strap
            because he insisted
on keeping the watch
            despite
its cloudy face.
            My father was
"Recycling
            Incarnate."
Except for the glittering
            dental work, he
expected his whole
            body to be
consumed
            in its new
life as science
            project—he willed it
to the Virginia
            Anatomical
Society!

            After Oliver Funeral
            Home arrived
to pick up "the

body," and I signed
off as Next
            of Kin,
I went to the nursing
            home guest room
and slept. Much later
            I was
nearly fully
            awakened by the
sense that my
            molar was loose,
then that my whole
            jaw had fallen
off and I could feel
            it throbbing,
pulsing on
            its own. I lay
in the dark
            in the phony Colonial
"guest suite" décor
            consumed by
terror over this thing
            that could
not be undone.

            Naïve freshman,
with little life as an
            artist, I was startled
by the horses laid out
            on Mr. Kern's floor. I
couldn't tell
            whether the
sprawled and bloated horses
            were dead or just
napping in their stalls, their bellies
            full after a night
grazing the lush summer
            grass.

HOW GOD IS LIKE A TRUFFLE

Like a goat
       in a stall
with a thoroughbred,
         a truffle sealed
in a plastic
     bag
with a dozen eggs
       or raw
uncooked
      rice. Like
an apple slice
      or piece
of bread shut
       away in an
airtight container
        with brown sugar—
or a small
       bowl of water
placed next to
      the hardened
lump
      and microwaved,
my god
     calms me,
flavors me, restores
      my softness. I tried
to explain to
      my husband
about the love
      animals have
for each
      other. How,
at Christy's,
      the donkey, Vinny,
herds and
      nibbles Love Bug,
white pony who wears
      an eye mask, who
just returned from
      cancer surgery. The

two of them
        in the sun.
The donkey
        nibbled my arm
too, but
        never bit. Don sat
across from
        me in my room
under a poster of van
        Gogh's *Yellow House*,
his eyes
        at half-mast.
He couldn't be
        less interested
in my "sacred."

        To be permeated
with God,
        I sit with him. I keep
a red zafu on
        the floor.
                Take
the waitlist
        letter for Lucy's
college, I said
        to my husband
and daughter
        this morning,
place it
        in a sealed
plastic bag
        with
an apple core or
        dried flower,
wait to open
        and there will
be the acceptance
        you have been
waiting for.

MY HOBBY NEEDED A HOBBY

My hobby needed a hobby you know how you get a dog and you have a dog
and then Kurt says we need to get the dog a puppy the dog needs somebody

to play with her to teach and then you have a baby bossy baby needs a little
baby and littler baby and then like you have a thing that you don't get paid

any money for it's like an art you do it for the love of it sooner or later
though it gets you know it starts to make you nervous you get caught up

in politics it doesn't matter that there's not any money it's prestige
rankings and who's up and who's down so that thing you were calling this

vocation the thing you did for art's sake you know you didn't want
to get paid for because you loved it so much it was like you loved

the work it felt like play I mean you looked up after several hours
you were so absorbed you didn't even know where the time went then it

gets onerous because this currency is being traded and you know it is starting
to get heavy it starts to be as heavy as coins people even use expressions

like coin of the realm my stock went up or my stock went down or somebody
or other didn't use their political capital all that kind of crap so now

your hobby your art needs a hobby that feels completely free and doesn't
have anything to do with the buying and selling attaching your worth to some

chips or tokens markers or whatever so you've got to get a new free thing
where you get completely absorbed and work feels like play well so I found

one my pet the pet little sister of my first pet is some horses well then I get
to the stable forget about time waste like five hours at a pop after a few years

start wearing a watch but am not going to worry yet so I am washing off
Berto the horse that I am helping to pay for but still it feels pretty free I don't

go to horse shows I'm like sixty-three years old people consider it a miracle
that I'm even staying on which I'm barely doing my trainer and I spend half

the time gossiping to the point where we decide we probably have to go
to lunch so I am washing Berto off and Berto is starting to squirm a little about

his pet out in the pasture he can just make out through the fence I can tell
he has a pet the horses all have buddies his pet is Vinny the donkey and when

I went to get him before my lesson he was chasing the red horses because
he thought they were bothering Vinny he does tolerate Love Bug the white pony

though because Love Bug is Vinny's little brother his inseparable companion
his familiar I go to get Berto he's in a herd of the black horses and one starts

to pin its ears and foment a little stampede but I yell my hateful yell and it stops
and Berto walks peacefully to the gate with me he acts sometimes like I'm his
    buddy

which makes me shine all over never mind the transactional aspect the treats and
carrots I'm loaded down with most of the time ban the word "transactional"

and also any consideration of the fantasy lovers mine and probably my husband's
not exactly pets or little brothers the priest tonight said we each have an angel

this is really the first I'd heard of it and I started picturing my crush
bathed in light oops no my angel I mean my real one though I don't think

it he she is my pet but more like I'm its I'm surrendered as somebody's distraction
from their day job their support poodle crossing buddy safe space spice cake

HIS CHEMIC BEAUTY

Your chemic beauty burned my muscles through. ——William Empson

Oh I don't know,
        I'm just not that enthusiastic

about eating meat anymore,
        my husband says, and I think

what is the weird
        visceral pull for me, sucking

on bones of an animal that
        recently ran around a barnyard

in the sun. Creepy. Pleasurable. Viscous.
        I eat some red rubbery burst

blood vessels, think fleetingly of lethal bacteria,
        salmonella, etc. I wrestled it raw on a cutting board,

trying to remember to use the special
        polyethylene one for meat we got when

I was switched onto this diet
        from pesce-ovotarian.

<   >

I stand between two cigarettes
        after the twelve-step meeting. Lucia's

and Raymond's. We're discussing
        Lucia's hypoglycemia. What they

had thought was gestational
        diabetes. I stand between two roses,

a man I loved once said. That's
        when I realized the woman on

the other side——Franny——was his new
girlfriend. I was frigging glad I didn't

get a chance with him. It would have
ruined my life! I saw him putting

a shine on eight-months-pregnant
Lucia, too. She came in the next week

with her hair all clean and falling around
her shoulders.

+ + +

I live my life between two

injections, one on Friday morning,
one on Monday. Which is not working too

well because each makes me sick.
I'm not fairy-dancing down

Vegetarian Lane anymore.
It's more like pan grease caramelized onions

and my mouth on the thigh bone
of someone who may have struggled

against the knife. Cleaved between the chemo
drug that "may cause lymphoma" and the

biologic that "may cause lymphoma,
rare blood cancers, neurological problems,

MS, heart failure, and death." And if you happen
to have some kind of sleeper

TB when you start taking the drug
or are unwittingly exposed to it,

you're toast. What I mean is I can't
        make it down the list of side effects

to grogginess, faint nausea, dizziness,
        brain fog, and a shitty headache. I get

stuck midway in the catalog, the dense black print on the
        pharmacist's warning sheet before me.

Forget the inch-thick package insert! "Site irritation"—
        the least of my worries, right?

> <

I live my life between two roses, my husband
        and this other man. Or my husband

as heterosexual and my husband as
        person with "homoerotic

desires"—or the two injections, their
        toxins coming at me through a needle from

two sides—I keep a chart of shot sites for each
        of my thighs—my elder daughter on

the upswing or the downward
        plunge of her bipolar, or my would-be

lover and his two would-be flowers. I gnaw
        the juicy bone of a recently

running-around chicken, the stubborn sinew,
        blood vessels in my teeth, gristle. Hyper-

plumped-up thigh meat I tear off with
        my cutting teeth, my incisors, but

it was raised in "humane conditions" and
        done in "gently"

with a head fake and a hatchet. I suck
    its fat its juice. It was between two roses.

POOL

I am suspended
    between
        two people.

My husband
    is nowhere
        present.

It's not really
    a competition
        because the man's

flopping
    and the woman uses a
        kickboard but

when she does
    the crawl
        she's twice as

fast as I
    am. I am
        suspended

between heaven
    and earth. Blue
        medium.

Backstroke is
    my favorite. I can
        see the

fluffy green trees
    waving at the
        top of the

hill. I try not to
    think of how
        just beyond

them, Kirk and Gale
used to
keep pool

passes
in a basket
on their

back porch. And how
they have
sold their

house and are
leaving for another
continent.

While I was trying to
grasp
child-rearing

they threw themselves
into it and now
abruptly out

of it. While I was looking
out a window
trying

to get a
bead on the
rituals of

high school (or
hiding from
them), they

were attending
every last soccer
game and

She Devil performance
      and documenting it all
            with copious

photographs, videos,
      etc. This is how
            it always

is. I am slow.
      I grip tight
            to stave

off the coming
      separation. Take
            this pool

for example. It's the
      noon fifty-
            minute

swim period.
      First, I was fifteen
            minutes

late because I thought
      it started at ten
            after; now

I'm thinking it's
      forever. This
            friendly

stasis, this
      welcoming
            truce. Always

going up and down
      the basement
            stairs

with the girls'
      laundry.
            Lucy's clothes

this time
      tortured by
            college dormitory

washers. They have
      two speeds:
            on and

off. I assiduously
      avoid the fact
            that all my

clothing rehab
      will be wrecked
            again

in September. The girl
      refuses to
            read labels! And

Eleanor—don't get
      me started.
            She is once

again preparing
      a dramatic
            European departure.

Lucy and I
      look at
            four fat-grip

vegetable peelers in
      arresting colors—
            was this

necessary? And the
        expensive eggs
                from the farmer's

market. And the dinner-
        planning getting
                more and more

elaborate. The three
        babysitting
                jobs back to

back, constant
        entertainment activities
                for the babies/

toddlers. Three pairs
        of Converse sneakers
                each received

and returned—she
        couldn't decide
                on the color. Lucy

looks up at
        me from
                another bag of

newly purchased kitchenware,
        dessert plates,
                deluxe

salad spinner—is
        she getting manic?
                We think

we know
        the answer. My husband
                is nowhere

present. He's on a road
        somewhere, supposedly
            headed this

way. He's been
        faraway refurbishing
            another house,

his mother's. He'll be
        back soon. Now
            if I could

only believe
        it. Believe that one
            of these

times when I
        slap my hand
            on the edge of

the pool, coming in
        for a sloppy landing,
            the sleepy-

haired guard will look at
        the clock on the
            wall over

by the office
        put the whistle to
            his mouth

and blow it.

About the Poet

Dana Roeser is the author of three previous books of poetry, *The Theme of Tonight's Party Has Been Changed* (University of Massachusetts Press), winner of the Juniper Prize, and *In the Truth Room* and *Beautiful Motion* (Northeastern University Press/UPNE), both winners of the Samuel French Morse Poetry Prize. Among her awards and honors are the Great Lakes Colleges Association New Writers Award (for *Beautiful Motion*), the Jenny McKean Moore Writer-in-Washington Fellowship, a National Endowment for the Arts Fellowship, a Pushcart Prize, and numerous residencies in the U.S. and abroad. She has read her work widely and taught in the MFA programs in poetry at Purdue, Butler, and Wichita State Universities. Please see www.danaroeser.com.

Publications by Two Sylvias Press:

The Daily Poet: Day-By-Day Prompts For Your Writing Practice
by Kelli Russell Agodon and Martha Silano (Print and eBook)

The Daily Poet Companion Journal (Print)

Fire On Her Tongue: An Anthology of Contemporary Women's Poetry
edited by Kelli Russell Agodon and Annette Spaulding-Convy (Print and eBook)

The Poet Tarot and Guidebook: A Deck Of Creative Exploration (Print)

All Transparent Things Need Thundershirts, Winner of the 2017 Two Sylvias Press Wilder Prize
by Dana Roeser (Print and eBook)

Where The Horse Takes Wing: The Uncollected Poems of Madeline DeFrees
edited by Anne McDuffie (Print and eBook)

In The House Of My Father
Winner of the 2017 Two Sylvias Press Chapbook Prize
by Hiwot Adilow (Print and eBook)

Box, Winner of the 2017 Two Sylvias Press Poetry Prize
by Sue D. Burton (Print and eBook)

Tsigan: The Gypsy Poem (New Edition)
by Cecilia Woloch (Print and eBook)

PR For Poets
by Jeannine Hall Gailey (Print and eBook)

Appalachians Run Amok, Winner of the 2016 Two Sylvias Press Wilder Prize
by Adrian Blevins (Print and eBook)

Pass It On!
by Gloria J. McEwen Burgess (Print)

Killing Marias
by Claudia Castro Luna (Print and eBook)

The Ego and the Empiricist, Finalist 2016 Two Sylvias Press Chapbook Prize
by Derek Mong (Print and eBook)

The Authenticity Experiment
by Kate Carroll de Gutes (Print and eBook)

Mytheria, Finalist 2015 Two Sylvias Press Wilder Prize
by Molly Tenenbaum (Print and eBook)

Arab in Newsland , Winner of the 2016 Two Sylvias Press Chapbook Prize
by Lena Khalaf Tuffaha (Print and eBook)

The Blue Black Wet of Wood, Winner of the 2015 Two Sylvias Press Wilder Prize
by Carmen R. Gillespie (Print and eBook)

Fire Girl: Essays on India, America, and the In-Between
by Sayantani Dasgupta (Print and eBook)

Blood Song
by Michael Schmeltzer (Print and eBook)

Naming The No-Name Woman,
Winner of the 2015 Two Sylvias Press Chapbook Prize
by Jasmine An (Print and eBook)

Community Chest
by Natalie Serber (Print)

Phantom Son: A Mother's Story of Surrender
by Sharon Estill Taylor (Print and eBook)

What The Truth Tastes Like
by Martha Silano (Print and eBook)

landscape/heartbreak
by Michelle Peñaloza (Print and eBook)

Earth, Winner of the 2014 Two Sylvias Press Chapbook Prize
by Cecilia Woloch (Print and eBook)

The Cardiologist's Daughter
by Natasha Kochicheril Moni (Print and eBook)

She Returns to the Floating World
by Jeannine Hall Gailey (Print and eBook)

Hourglass Museum
by Kelli Russell Agodon (eBook)

Cloud Pharmacy
by Susan Rich (eBook)

Dear Alzheimer's: A Caregiver's Diary & Poems
by Esther Altshul Helfgott (eBook)

Listening to Mozart: Poems of Alzheimer's
by Esther Altshul Helfgott (eBook)

Crab Creek Review 30th Anniversary Issue featuring Northwest Poets edited by Kelli Russell
Agodon and Annette Spaulding-Convy (eBook)

Please visit Two Sylvias Press (www.twosylviaspress.com) for information on purchasing our print
books, eBooks, writing tools, and for submission guidelines for our annual book prizes.

The Wilder Series Poetry Book Prize

The Wilder Series Book Prize is an annual contest hosted by Two Sylvias Press. It is open to women over 50 years of age (established or emerging poets) and includes a $1000 prize, publication by Two Sylvias Press, 20 copies of the winning book, and a vintage, art nouveau pendant. Women submitting manuscripts may be poets with one or more previously published chapbooks/books or poets without any prior chapbook/book publications. The judges for the prize are Two Sylvias Press cofounders and coeditors, Kelli Russell Agodon and Annette Spaulding-Convy.

The Wilder Series Book Prize draws its inspiration from American author, Laura Ingalls Wilder, who published her first *Little House* book at age 65 and completed the last manuscript in the series at age 76. Wilder's autobiography, which she wrote in her late 60s, was published in 2014, after having been rejected in the 1930s by editors due to its "inappropriate" and "mature" material. Two Sylvias Press is proud to introduce a poetry series featuring women over age 50—young women may be wild, but mature women are *wilder*.

To learn more about submitting to the Wilder Prize, please visit:
http://twosylviaspress.com/wilder-series-poetry-book-prize.html

The Wilder Series Book Prize Winners and Finalists

2017:
Dana Roeser, *All Transparent Things Need Thundershirts* (Winner)

2016:
Adrian Blevins, *Appalachians Run Amok* (Winner)

2015:
Carmen R. Gillespie, *The Blue Black Wet of Wood* (Winner)
Molly Tenenbaum, *Mytheria* (Finalist)